THE SUSTAINABLE JOY OF STORING, CANNING, DRYING, AND FERMENTING

RALEIGH BRIGGS

MICROCOSM PUBLISHING
Portland, OR | Cleveland, OH

SAVE YOUR FOOD
The Sustainable Joy of Storing, Canning, Drying, and Fermenting

ISBN 9781648417511
This is Microcosm #981

For a catalog, write or visit:
Microcosm Publishing
2752 N Williams Ave.
Portland, OR 97227
All the news from the misfts in print at www.Microcosm.Pub/Newsletter

Find more zines at www.Microcosm.Pub/Zines
Get more copies of this book at www.Microcosm.Pub/SaveYourFood
Get more from the author at www.Microcosm.Pub/Raleigh
Find more books like this at www.Microcosm.pub/GoodLife

To join the ranks of high-class stores that feature Microcosm titles, talk to your rep: In the U.S. COMO (Atlantic), ABRAHAM (Midwest), sales@microcosm.pub (Texas, Oklahoma, Arkansas, Louisiana), IMPRINT (Pacific), TURNAROUND (UK, Africa, Europe, Middle East), UTP/MANDA (Canada), NEWSOUTH (Australia/New Zealand), APD (Asia), HarperCollins (India), and FAIRE in the gift trade.

Did you know that you can buy our books directly from us at sliding scale rates? Support a small, independent publisher and pay less than Amazon's price at **www.Microcosm.Pub**.

Global labor conditions are bad, and our roots in industrial Cleveland in the '70s and '80s made us appreciate the need to treat workers right. Therefore, our books are MADE IN THE USA.

EU Safety Information: microcosmpublishing.com/gpsr

MICROCOSM PUBLISHING is Portland's most diversified publishing house and distributor, with a focus on the colorful, authentic, and empowering. Our books and zines have put your power in your hands since 1996, equipping readers to make positive changes in their lives and in the world around them. Microcosm emphasizes skill-building, showing hidden histories, and fostering creativity through challenging conventional publishing wisdom with books and bookettes about DIY skills, food, bicycling, gender, self-care, and social justice. What was once a distro and record label started by Joe Biel in a drafty bedroom was determined to be *Publishers Weekly*'s fastest-growing publisher of 2022 and #3 in 2023 and 2024, and is now among the oldest independent publishing houses in Portland, OR, and Cleveland, OH. We are a politically moderate, centrist publisher in a world that has inched to the right for the past 80 years.

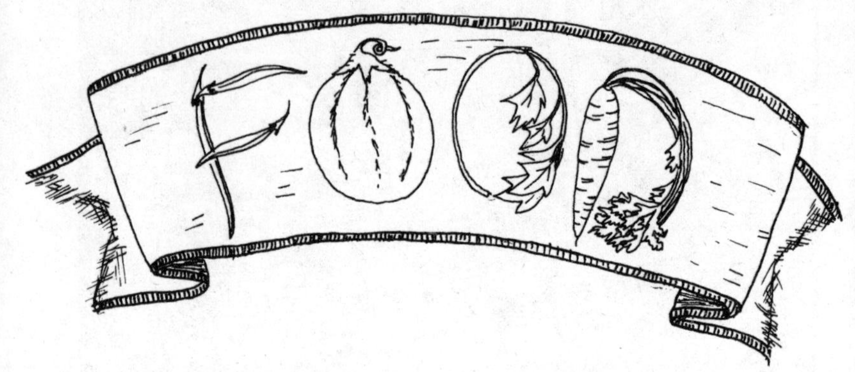
FOOD

You know what's awesome? Growing food. And eating food. What's not quite as awesome? Figuring out what to do with the 50 lbs of zucchini getting flabby in your fridge. Never fear! This chapter is all about what to do with those delicious windfalls.

A lot of these processes will be familiar to many of you. Canning in particular is having a resurgence, and for good reason. It's really fun, delicious, and makes for great socializing if your friends are willing to help. That's the gift of DIY: it gives you a shared experience that lasts a lot longer than the quick buzz of a trip to the supermarket.

NOTE: Please play it safe whenever you're preserving food. That means using fresh ingredients, keeping everything clean, sterilizing equipment when you need to, and paying extra attention to food temperatures. Some of the processes in this chapter can take a long time, but cutting the steps short can lead to food that's unsafe to eat. Use your best judgement!

♡ Take care of yourself and each other. ♡

Storing Veggies

If you've ever tended a garden, you know that some years you might harvest nothing but three seedy, shrimpy cucumbers; other years, you might end up with more warty heirloom squashes than you know what to do with. It's the blessing and curse of every home garden. It's okay, though—if you're having a bountiful year and all your neighbors are *sick of your damn zucchini*, there are still plenty of ways to keep your harvest fresh until you eat it.

Preplanning Tips

Be realistic about what you can eat. It's fun to try new things in your garden, but if you're sowing a high-yield crop, take a moment to consider whether you'd be willing to eat it a couple times a week. Doesn't sound so appealing? Consider bartering or donating your excess veggies.

Make your own veggie dungeon. For a few of these methods, it helps to have a root cellar or something of that ilk, but any dark, well-ventilated space will work. Your veggies need to be kept away from heat and light, and many of them need a little humidity to keep them from withering. If you have a dark cabinet or other space, install a thermometer inside so you can monitor the temperature, and make sure there aren't any heating vents or heat sources nearby. If you're planning to store plants that like a little humidity (like carrots and turnips), you might want to add a humidifier or a few slightly damp towels that you can regularly replace and check for mildew.

Clean out your freezer or root cellar before you harvest. Any storage prep or preservation should happen as soon as possible after the plant is picked to preserve the fresh flavor and helpful enzymes of the food.

Harvesting

Handle with care. Fresh fruits and veggies are delicate, and unblemished specimens will store much better than bruised ones. Use a light touch to pick and clean your harvest, and throw out anything that's moldy or buggy.

Give underground-dwellers a little light. When onions, garlic, potatoes, and other below-ground edibles are dug up, their skins are still moist. Storing these freshly dug can lead to rot and mold. Instead, dig up these foods on a dry, sunny day and let them sit on the surface of the garden for a few hours afterwards. This will help their skins harden a bit, which will help them stay mold-free for longer.

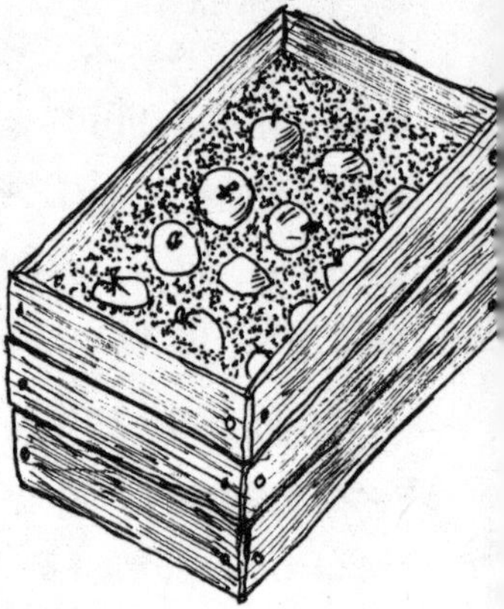

Storing Produce

Crate apples, pears, + roots

Most hardy fruits can be stored in wooden boxes on the shelf of your root cellar or storage area. The key here is to keep the pieces from touching each other, to protect the fruit from rot or fungus. One way to accomplish this is to wrap each piece in waxed paper, parchment, or even newspaper. Pack them in a single layer, pad with crumpled paper, and repeat. If you're more ambitious, you can swap the paper for barely moist sand or dry sawdust.

The sand/sawdust route also works for carrots, beets, and other roots. Brush any excess dirt off the roots first (don't wash them), and lop off the greens to keep them from pulling nutrients from the root. Make a thin layer of sand on the bottom of the crate, then lay down a layer of roots, making sure the roots don't touch each other. Add sand around and onto the roots, and repeat.

Hang pumpkins, squash, onions, and garlic

Easy and fun! You can get really creative with your hanging techniques (garlic garlands!), but storing these long-storing veggies can be as simple as dropping the bulbs or squashes into an old pair of stockings, tying a knot between each bulb to keep them from touching, and then hanging the whole shebang up in your root cellar. If it doesn't look nice enough, use prettier stockings. :)

Bag potatoes

Potatoes keep well in a plain old paper bag, as long as the humidity is kept as low as possible AND they're kept away from light. If you live in a humid climate, you can cure your potatoes first by letting their skins toughen in the sun for a few hours before you store them. Don't wash before you bag —just brush off the excess dirt with your hand or with a dry brush. If you're worried about sprouting, toss an apple in the bag with the potatoes. It works, somehow.

Dry beans, fruits, mushrooms, peppers, and tomatoes

Drying a food obviously alters its appearance and texture, so it's not ideal for every purpose, but dried food does last a really long time. It saves space and weight in your pantry, kitchen, backpack, or whatever.

I'm not going to include instructions for dehydrators here, because I don't own one. I'm sure it's a lovely tool to have, but it's not absolutely necessary. All you really need is an oven, some counter space, and a day or two to let the process happen.

Maybe you're thinking: "doy, Raleigh, why can't I just leave my fruit in the sun?" Well, you can. It just takes longer, and you need reliably dry, sunny weather the whole time. So if you know you're gonna have a week without a cloud in the sky, go for it. Otherwise, use your oven like so:

Bean pods should stay on the plant until they're yellow and brittle. Then, cut down the whole plant and hang it up until it's completely dry. Sort through all the dry foliage, pull the beans out of their pods and let them dry indoors on baking sheets for a few more days. From there, you can pour them into airtight containers and keep around until burrito day.

Fruits (including tomatoes) are best dried in a warm oven (between 110 and 130° F). Slice apples and pears thinly. Berries and seedless grapes can be halved (if large). Tomatoes and stone fruits should be halved (and pitted, if applicable). Whatever you've got, spread it out on a baking sheet, sprinkle with sugar (optional—use salt for tomatoes) and dry in that warm oven for a day or so.

The fruit is ready to store when it looks and feels dry. You shouldn't be able to squeeze any juice out of it. Once it's fully dehydrated, keep the fruit in airtight jars. Eat it as-is, bake with it, or reconstitute it in a little boiling water.

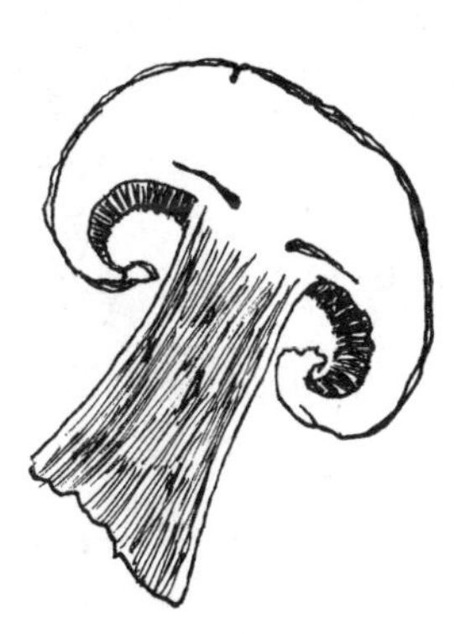

Mushrooms can be dried the same way as fruit (skip the sugar). Slice the bigger mushrooms and keep the little ones whole. You can also use a needle and cotton thread to string sturdier mushrooms onto a garland and hang them up to dry. Cute!

Peppers can be dried like fruit in a 140° oven, OR you can string them up in bunches and let them dry in a warm, ventilated area.

Freeze peas, beans, corn, and other delicates

Spring and summer's eager, plentiful veggies don't store well, so freezing is a good option. As soon as possible after your harvest, create a little assembly line like so: Have a big pot of water boiling on the stove; a bowl of ice water close by; a colander by the sink; and a baking sheet on the counter.

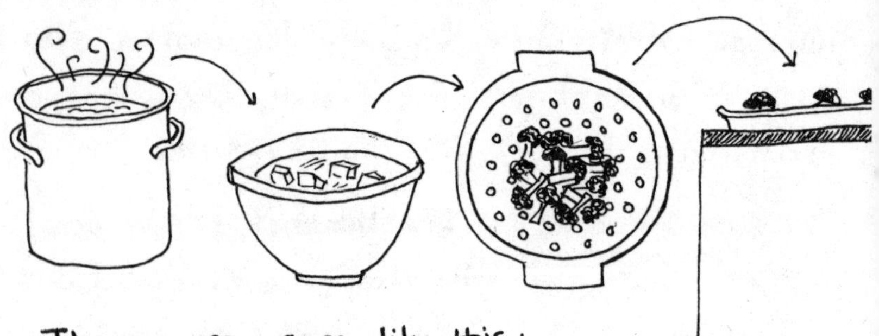

The process goes like this:

Step 1: Clean and prep a small batch of veggies.

Step 2: Blanch the veggies in water for 1-2 minutes. For bigger chunks like broccoli florets, blanch a little longer. Corn on the cob should boil for at least 5 minutes.

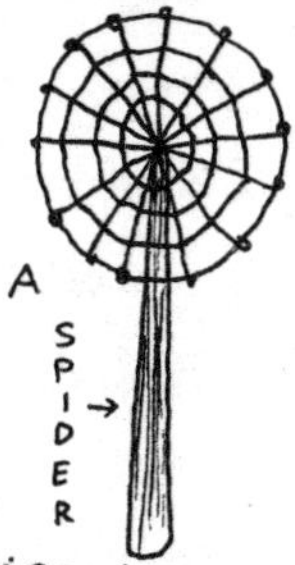

Step 3: Using a spider, tongs, or a slotted spoon, remove the veggies from the boiling water and dunk them into the ice water.

A
S
P
I
D
E
R →

Step 4: While the first batch is cooling, prep the second batch and add those veggies to the boiling pot. Start your timer!

Step 5: Remove the veggies from the ice bath and let them drain in the colander.

Step 6: Continue like this until all the veggies have been blanched and cooled. Dry the veggies in the colander with a towel and then spread them on the baking sheet in a single layer.

Step 7: Pop the baking sheet in the freezer. This will allow each chunk of vegetable matter to freeze separately, eliminating any clumpy masses of frozen crap later. Once frozen, pop everything in plastic bags and label them.

Clamp a ton of root vegetables

Do you have mild winters and a veritable buttload of root vegetables? Congrats! Clamping might be your jam. A clamp is very literally a food pyramid, created outside and covered with earth and straw. This is a little impractical for most people, but if you have a large garden (or a small farm), it's a great, traditional way to store tons of food without encroaching on anyone's living space.

To make a clamp, you'll need a bare patch of ground and loose, dry-ish soil, plus a shovel and some dry straw. Harvest your roots and let them sit on top of the ground while you site and start building your clamp.

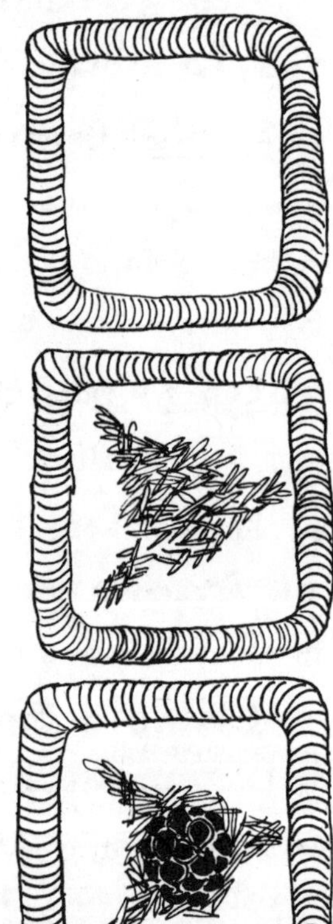

Step 1: Pick a spot that tends to stay dry (under an eave is good), and dig a trench around the area to keep the clamp site from getting soggy.

Step 2: Make a nice layer of straw for your veggies to rest on. Add a couple of "legs" to the straw layer by building little tunnels outward from the main pile.

Step 3: Pile the roots on top in a mound shape and cover with more straw. Let the clamp sit for 24-48 hours to allow any moisture from the roots to evaporate.

Step 4: Using a small shovel or spade, pile earth on top of the clamp. Leave the legs uncovered — they'll act as vents to keep air circulating around the roots. Build the clamp in a pyramid shape until you've added about 5 inches of dirt on every side.

Step 5: Pack the top layer down nicely and keep the walls steep so that any rain that hits it will roll right off.

AND NOW YOU HAVE A CLAMP!

Crap! My carrots have gone limp. ῆ

★ To revive flabby vegetables like carrots, celery, potatoes, or lettuce, wash what you've got and then soak those suckers in ice water + 1 T vinegar for up to an hour. Should be firm and sprightly by then.

drying herbs

Drying herbs is a simple, effective way to preserve most of their taste, color, and medicinal properties. Dried herbs might not taste exactly like fresh ones, but in the middle of winter a little bit of summery flavor goes a long way.

As for process, you've got a veritable glut of options. But you'll want to start by:

Prepping Herbs for Drying

* Harvest herbs when your plants are preparing to blossom. The plant's leaves will be full of essential oils, which is what you want.

* The best time to gather herbs is in the morning after the day's dew has evaporated. Mid to late summer is perfect, because the days will be warm and dry and most leafy herbs will be at their peak.

* Herbs should be cleaned carefully to avoid scrubbing off any aromatic oils. A rinse in cold water will do the trick. Afterwards, gently shake the herbs and let them air dry completely. Pick off any dead or gross leaves and compost them.

* Once your herbs are dry, they should be stored in an airtight container away from light, heat, and humidity. You can crush them or keep them whole.

Bunch Drying → for herbs with lengthy stems

Step 1: Snip and wash your herbs.

Step 2: While the herbs are air-drying, grab a paper bag and open it up. Use a pokey instrument (knitting needle? BBQ skewer?) to punch several holes in each side of the bag.

Step 3: Bundle your herbs and tie the stems together with twine. Stick the tops of the herbs inside the bag and gather the top of the bag around the stems. Secure the top of the bag with more twine.

Step 4: Hang the whole contraption somewhere warm, well-ventilated, and away from direct sunlight. (The doorway of your kitchen might be perfect.) The bag is optional, honestly, but it will provide further sun protection and keep the herbs from getting dusty.

Flat Drying → for seeds + herbs with short stems

Step 1: Prep, wash, and dry your herbs.

Step 2: Lay the herbs in a single layer on a baking sheet (or two). Cover the herbs with a clean tea towel and place the tray in a warm area where it won't be disturbed.

Step 3: Stir the herbs every few days to make sure they're drying evenly.

Cool Oven

↳ for large quantities of herbs + for impatient people

Follow steps 1 + 2 of the flat drying method. The warm place you'll use will be your oven, heated to only ~ 180°F. Prop the oven door open a little and leave the herbr there for a few hours. Stir the herbs gently every hour to make sure they're not sticking, scorching, or drying unevenly.

Even Cooler Oven → for non-bakers

* NOTE: Needs a gas oven

Follow the directions for the cool oven method, but don't turn the oven on. Leave the herbs in there for a day

or two and the pilot light will dry them out.

NOTE: This method obviously works best if you don't bake a lot. Make sure to take the herbs out of your oven before you use it or else: scorch city.

Microwave → for woody herbs

Step 1: Spread clean, ABSOLUTELY DRY herbs on a paper towel.

Step 2: Nuke the herbs on high for 1 minute. If the leaves are still supple, nuke for 30 seconds more.

Step 3: Repeat step 2 until the leaves are dry and brittle. Let them cool on the counter.

NOTE: You really have to do this 30 seconds at a time to prevent *fire* and *scorching*. BE PATIENT!

Freezing → for when drying won't cut it

Dry basil or cilantro will do in an absolute culinary emergency, but let's face it: they suck. So what's a gardener to do? Freeze those suckers fresh + preserve that flava. After you prep, chop the herbs + freeze them in a single layer on a baking sheet.

OR! Blend the herbs with a little water, broth, or oil and put one teaspoon in each section of an ice cube tray for pre-measured herbs at the ready!

Tangent: one of my first forays into DIY herbal work involved sticking a few sprigs of sage into an old bottle of vinegar from the kitchen. I didn't eat a lot of salad back then (I was a teenager), but I used it in my bathwater + on my zitty face and it was just fabulous. Herbal vinegars: so simple even a 15-year-old idiot can make them. Anyway.

Herbal vinegars capture the flavor of an herb in a tasty, shelf-stable liquid form. They're perfect for using in marinades, vinaigrettes, or on fresh fruit. Or, as my story suggests, you can use them for cosmetic or medicinal applications.

To make herbal vinegar, all you need to do is infuse a good quality vinegar with fresh herbs and let it steep in a dark place for about a month so all the flavors of your concoction can blend. Then, strain out the solids and let it sit for another week or two until the flavors are pleasingly mellow.

The proportion of herbs to vinegar is important, but it's not set in stone. Start with a <u>few big sprigs of fresh herb</u> per <u>cup of vinegar</u>, and let it steep for a couple of weeks. If it still tastes weak, you can add a bit more.

The type of vinegar you use depends on what you're using the finished product for. Apple cider vinegar is full of nutrients and is perfect for cosmetic and medicinal blends, but the taste is a little too strong for most people. White wine, red wine, sherry, and rice vinegars are great bases for culinary herbs.

Herbal Vinegar Ideas

★ white wine vinegar + chives, sage, thyme, or rosemary (+ lemon peel?)

★ red wine vinegar + basil or oregano, or really any Italian herb

★ sherry vinegar + tarragon or ramps

★ apple cider vinegar + fresh raspberries or strawberries

HOT TIP: Want something a little stronger? Swap the vinegar for decent vodka, brandy, whiskey, or rum. Steep for a month, strain, then make into cocktails that cost $10 each.

Herbal Syrups & Honeys

True fact: An herb-spiked simple syrup or honey will take your next batch of cocktails to the NEXT LEVEL. Also going to the next level: lemonade, iced tea, soda water, pound cake, and anything else that calls for a glaze or liquid sweetener.

Herbal syrups are super easy to make, and the recipe multiplies well, so you can whip up a batch whether you have bushels of herbs or just a few sprigs. So next time you find some extra-fragrant rosemary growing on the sidewalk, grab it—you won't regret it!

Basic Herbal Syrup

1 cup sweetener, like sugar or agave

1 cup water

A dozen or so herb sprigs, or a big hand-

-ful of fresh leaves.

<u>Step 1</u>: Stir water and sugar together in a small saucepan and bring to a boil on the stove. Stir until all the sugar is dissolved. If sugar crystals form on the sides of the pan, wet them down with a wet pastry brush.

<u>Step 2</u>: Add the herbs and crush them into the pan with your spoon. (Don't bruise them with your hands — you want the oils to release into the sugar mixture, not onto your hands.) Cover the pot, and let the herbs steep for up to an hour.

<u>Step 3</u>: Using a sieve and a funnel, strain your syrup into a jar or a bottle with a tight-fitting lid. Leave an inch or so of headspace in the jar, in case you decide to freeze the syrup later. Press the remaining herbs with your spoon to get the last drops of syrup out, then toss the herbs in the compost bin.

★ herbs to try ★

- ★ rosemary
- ★ thyme
- ★ rose petal
- ★ violet
- ★ lavender
- ★ lemon verbena

<u>Step 4</u>: Label your syrup! This will keep for up to a month in the fridge or a year in the freezer.

Herbal Honey

2 cups light-flavored honey, like clover

1 tablespoon of fresh herbs, ground well
(or you could use 1 teaspoon dried)

Cheesecloth

Step 1: Wash and prep your herbs, then tie them up in the cheesecloth.

Step 2: Put the honey and herbs into a heavy-bottomed pot and warm it over low heat. If you're using raw honey, heat the honey only until it's warm.

Step 3: Pour the whole shebang into a mason jar, seal it up, and let it sit in a dark place for two weeks (longer for more intensely flavored honey).

Step 4: Heat the honey again; remove the herbs and squeeze out any honey. Strain the honey back into the jar.

Herbal Blend Ideas

- ★ For tea parties: lavender, rose petal, or fennel seed
- ★ For colds: lemon balm, rosemary, or mint
- ★ For bedtime: chamomile or lavender

Canning

Canning is arguably the most popular form of food preservation right now, and for good reason: homemade pickles, preserves, and jams are among the most delicious things you'll ever eat. I am completely biased. But if you grow great produce or know where to find it, there's nothing more rewarding than being able to save those perfect berries and incredible vegetables for a dark, dreary winter day.

Also, people freak out over homemade jam, and pickling parties are really fun. So there's that.

I'm only providing a couple basic recipes in this book, because there are hundreds of canning books out there right now. You might notice I'm only talking about jams, jellies, and pickles, and not including stuff like canned meat or non-pickled veggies. That's because those foods can't be canned safely without a pressure canner, which can heat food to a higher temperature than a

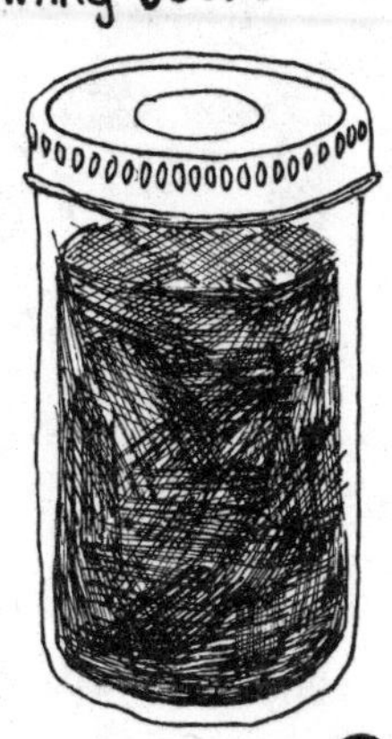

pot of boiling water can. This section is mainly for beginners, so pressure-canner recipes are a bit out of scope.

Supplies

You can find tons of tools that purport to make canning less labor-intensive, but the truth is that it's a long process no matter what. Unless you're starting a jam business, I suggest you start with the basics. And here they are!

A Cooking Pot: Use a big, heavy-bottomed pot (6–8 quarts) that's wide enough to cover your stove's largest burner. Material is important here: pickles, jams, and preserves all require some kind of acid, so a non-reactive pot is essential. Choose stainless steel or enamel and you're good to go.

A Boiling Pot: This mother needs to be BIG, at least 9 quarts, and bigger if you plan on canning large or multiple batches at once. Make sure it's deep, too, so that the jars can be completely covered without causing any boilover.

There needs to be some kind of rack in the bottom of the boiling pot to keep the jars from bumping around. You can buy a rack, or you can improvise by adding a metal trivet or folded dish-towel to the pot before you fill it up.

Jars, Rings, and Lids: Use Mason or Ball jars, *not* old pickle or mayo jars from the store. That will end in tragedy, or at least failure.

Canning jars are easy to find at grocery or thrift stores. Rings and jars in good condition are fine to reuse, but buy new flat lids each time you can. Once you crack the seal on a jar of home-canned food, the lid can't be reused. Sorry. :(

Other Tools, in no particular order:

★ a jar lifter (sooo much nicer than tongs!)

★ a wide-mouth funnel

★ a sieve (if you're making jelly)

★ a candy thermometer

★ a kitchen scale

★ a wooden spoon

★ a chopstick

★ a ladle

★ a small, heatproof bowl

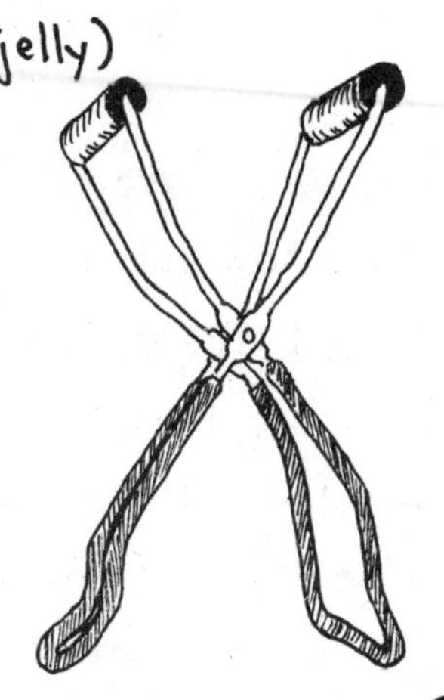

The Process goes like this:

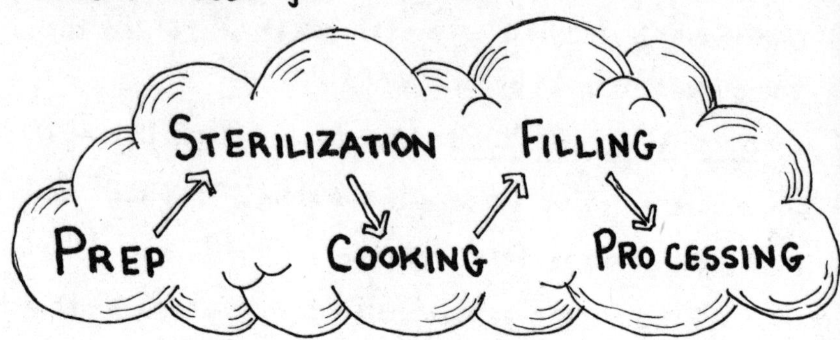

Step 1: Prep your fruit or veggies. If you're making jam, this might mean hulling strawberries or pitting apricots. For pickles, it might entail lots of chopping. Either way, get it done with and have your ingredients prepped and measured ahead of time.

Step 2: Start your hot water bath for later on. Fill the boiling pot with water, add the jar rack, and put it on the stove over high heat.

Step 3: Wash your jars, rings, and lids. Place the lids in a heatproof bowl, and have the rings next to them on the counter. Place the clean jars on a folded towel (we'll call it a prep towel) near the boiling pot. While you're at it, put another folded towel (the cooling towel) nearby to hold the jars after they come out of the water bath. Grab the jar lifter, funnel, ladle, and chopstick, and have them nearby, too.

Step 4: If your recipe calls for a processing time of 10 minutes or less, sterilize your jars before you fill them. Once the water boils, use a jar lifter to put the jars in one by one. Keep them submerged for at least 10 minutes.

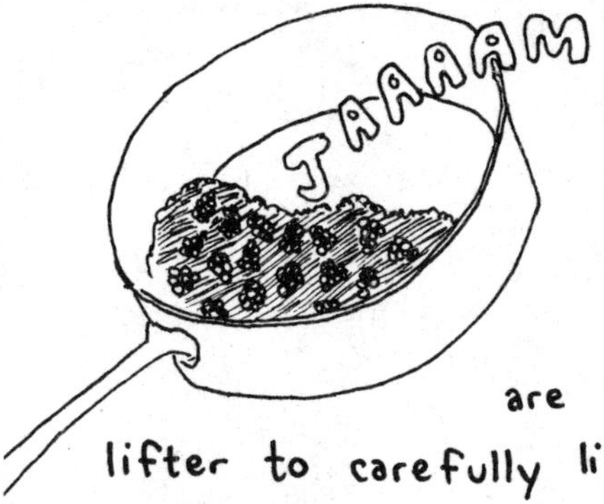

Step 5: Make your preserves, pickles, or whatever delights you have in store.

Step 6: When the jars are sterilized, use the jar lifter to carefully lift the first jar out of the water bath. Pour the water from this jar into the heatproof bowl, on top of the jar lids. A warm bath will soften the rubber on these guys and help form a tight seal later on. Remove the remaining jars from the water bath, tip the water from each into the pot, and place them on the prep towel.

Step 7: Using the ladle and funnel, pour your brine or jam into the hot jars. Leave about 1/4" of headspace in each jar (this might vary by recipe).

Once the jars are full, run the chopstick around the inside of each jar to remove any large air bubbles. Wipe each jar's rim with a damp towel.

Step 8: Plop a warm jar lid on each jar. Add the ring and screw it on until it's just tight—don't force it! A lid that's too tight will trap any lingering air bubbles inside, which is bad news.

Use the jar lifter to place the jars upright in the water bath. The water should cover the jars by at least an inch or two. Boil away for the length of time designated in your recipe. Then, lift the jars out and place them on the cooling towel.

Step 9: Leave these babies alone for an hour or two, then do a pop test on each lid to make sure it sealed properly. If the lid pops up and down when you press it with a finger, your jar isn't sealed. Ain't no thing, though: you

can still stick the jar in the fridge and use what's in it. It's just not shelf-stable.

Once the jars have cooled completely, remove the rings and store the jars in a cool, dark place. Why remove the rings? To detect botulism, of course! Dangerous bacteria get very active in an environment like a poorly sealed jar. If your jar has nasties in it and the ring's off, the pressure inside will force the lid to pop off. Thus, you know not to eat whatever's in there. Better messy than sick, amiright?

★ ★ ★

★ Simple No-Pectin Jam

★ makes ~ 2 quarts

4 lbs clean (peeled, seeded) chopped fruit

4 c sugar

4 T lemon juice (little less if your fruit is tart)

Pour all your ingredients into the cooking pot. If the fruit isn't super juicy, add 1/4 - 1/2 c water. Cook this mess over medium-low heat for about 2 hours, or until the temperature on a candy thermometer reads 220°F. At this point, your fruit will look suspiciously like jam. To test it, put a dollop on a saucer and stick it in the fridge. After a few minutes of chilling, the jam should be soft but not runny. If it's runny, cook another 15 minutes or so.

Ladle the jam into hot, sterilized jars, leaving about 1/4" headspace. Close up the jars like we talked about and process them in a water bath for 5 minutes to seal the jars.

Green Bean or Asparagus Pickles

*makes ~2 quarts

2 lbs clean, trimmed asparagus or green beans

4 cloves peeled garlic
1 bunch fresh dill
4 t kosher salt
2 1/2 c cider vinegar
2 1/2 c water
1/2 - 1 t chile flakes

Blanch the veggies + pack them into jars. Add a garlic clove and a couple dill sprigs to each ^sterilized! jar.

Bring the rest of the ingredients to a boil over high heat. Using a ladle, pour the hot brine over the pickles, submerging them + leaving 1/4" headspace.

Close up the jars and process for 10 minutes in a water bath.

Lacto-Fermentation

This method of preservation isn't quite as popular as canning, but perhaps it should be. Rather than using heat to kill off bacteria, lacto-fermentation uses bacteria to preserve food. The result is tangy, pickle-esque veggies and fruits bursting with healthful microbes. So all you kombucha freaks, pay attention: this one's for you!

The keys to successful fermentation are salt, time, and compression. The process is anaerobic, so you don't even need air—in fact air will only spoil the fun. You'll also need some tools you might not already have. The ideal fermenting vessel is a stoneware crock with a lid that can fit tightly inside it. You can find one in a specialty store or online.

Other equipment you'll need: a large rock to weigh down the lid, a large bowl, a sharp knife, and a large cutting board.

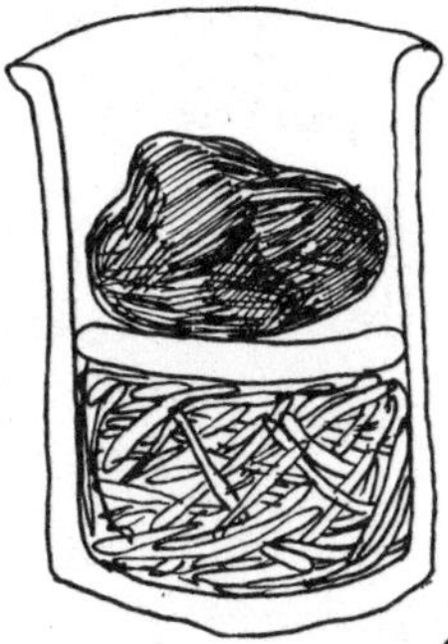

The most popular dishes prepared this way includ sauerkraut and kimchi, but you can lacto-ferment all sor of fruits, veggies, and even beverages. Give it a try!

Sauerkraut *makes 3 quarts*

5 lbs cabbage
3 T kosher salt

Before you start, boil a big pot of water, scrub the rock you're using, and boil it for a few minute Take it out and let it cool while you work.

Core the cabbage and slice it thinly. Place it in a large bowl and toss it with the salt.

Working a handful at a time, pack the cabbage into the crock. Really mash it in there! Once it's all in, smush the lid down on top of it and add the rock on top of that. Cover everything with a tea towel and move it out of the way.

Each day, push down on the rock to keep the cabbage tightly packed. Liquid will rise up aroun the lid, and that's great! It's just water drawn ou by the salt. As long as the cabbage stays totally submerged in this brine, you're golden.

Let the cabbage ferment for two weeks. After about a week, try removing the lid and peek inside. You might see some bubbles or gross floaty spots. As long as these are on top of the liquid and not on the actual cabbage, there's no reason to freak. Skim off what you can and replace the lid and rock.

When two weeks are up, remove the kraut and put it into clean 1-quart jars. Keep these in the fridge and they'll last quite a while. Enjoy!

Lacto-Fermented Dill Pickles

★makes 2 quarts★

sour + salty — not vinegary!

10-12 pickling cukes, scrubbed and trimmed
2 T mustard seeds
1 T whole black peppercorns
4 big sprigs fresh dill
4 T sea salt
2 c spring water
2 grape leaves (optional — they preserve crispness)

Layer the ingredients in a fermenting crock. Make sure the water covers the pickles. Add the lid and rock on top (see Sauerkraut recipe). Let the pickles ferment for up to a week. Then, transfer them to the fridge packed in 1-quart jars. Again, you might notice a few bubbles here and there, but you're good as long as the pickles stay submerged. Your pickles will keep for up to 3 months in the fridge.

Making Jerky

I'm not going to ask why you have that much meat in your fridge. Maybe there was a sale. Maybe you and your friends bought a pasture-raised cow together + now your freezer's brimming with odd cuts you don't know what to do with. Maybe you found it! It doesn't matter. If you have lots of meat, make jerky. It's delicious, nutritious, and keeps long enough for you to actually finish it.

When choosing meat for jerky, pick a lean cut. The fat in meat is what turns rancid first, so fatty cuts of meat = nasty jerky. Big animals (cows, deer, elk) are popular for making jerky, but turkey and salmon work great, too.

Step 1: Using a sharp knife, trim as much fat as you can from your meat.

Step 2: Put a little bit of water or marinade in a pot and add the meat. Bring the liquid to a simmer and braise the meat until it's cooked through. Stick a meat thermometer in the pot to make sure beef, game, and fish reach 160°F;

Chicken, turkey, and other poultry should reach 180°F.

If you're wondering about why we cook meat before drying: while drying meat inactivates many harmful organisms, it doesn't kill them. They'll still be milling around in your meat until you cook it.

Anyway, once the meat is cooked, drain it and let it cool. Preheat your oven to 175°F.

Step 3: Place the meat on a clean cutting board. Use a sharp knife to cut the meat into thin strips (no thicker than ¼"). Spread the meat on a baking sheet or two.

Step 4: Add seasoning! Salt at the very least, but I urge you to try out different spices, sugars, chiles, and citrus juices to see what tickles your fancy.

Step 5: Pop the meat in the oven, leaving the door slightly ajar, and cook the meat for about 5 hours. Successful jerky will be shriveled, dark, and firm but pliable enough to bend without snapping.

Step 6: Let the meat rest on paper towels to drain off any fat. When it's completely cool, keep the jerky in an airtight container for up to 2 months. Toss it out if it looks or smells moldy.

SALT-CURING FISH

These days, we tend to freeze food when we want to keep it on hand for a long time. Freezing is convenient, of course, but it's also a major trade-off. If you've ever defrosted a salmon filet to find it tasteless and dry, you know what I mean. A possible solution? Go super old-fashioned and try your hand at salt-curing.

Salt has been used to preserve food for basically ever. Packing meat and fish in salt (or alternately, soaking it in a brine solution) not only preserves the food, but infuses it with more flavor and a lovely firm texture.

Not gonna lie: this is a lengthy process. But if you like to fish or you participate in a CSA-style program, salt-curing will come in really handy when you suddenly have more fishes than one freezer can handle. You might say curing is really worth its salt! (But I won't.)

A few notes before you begin:

★ See if you can cure your fish in the summer, because you'll need plenty of sunshine and fresh air.

★ Salt curing, much like freezing, can affect the texture of your food. Salt draws moisture out of food, so salt-cured fish will be very firm and flaky Plenty of people love this texture, but it may not be your thing. I say give it a try — if you don't like it, someone else surely well.

★ For salt-cure recipes, most folks use curing salt, which has large crystals that can soak up a lot of moisture. If you can find curing salt near you, awesome. If not, substitute any chunky or flaky salt, preferably one without additives like iodine. You'll need a lot of it (1lb salt for every 5 lbs fish so choose something you can afford several large boxes of.

Coarse kosher salt is a terrific choice, as is Alaea salt or coarse sea salt.

Equipment:

* fresh fish (sans heads, guts, and blood, and filleted off the bone)
* lots of salt—see notes
* a cooler or other large watertight container
* a baking sheet or large, flat-bottomed bowl
* a large, clean bucket for rinsing
* clean wooden planks and non-metal weights
  - for smaller jobs, you can use dishes instead of planks
* a wooden clothes-drying rack or other wood frame

PHASE 1: THE SALTING

Step 1: If you need to, sort your fish by type—you'll need to preserve each type of fish separately.

Step 2: Coat the bottom of your cooler with a thin, even layer of salt. Grab a baking sheet or flat-bottomed bowl and pour a bunch of salt in that, too.

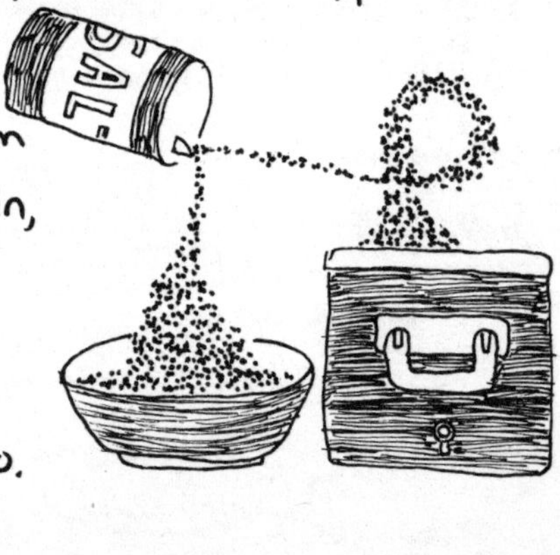

Step 3: Plop each piece of fish into the bowl or baking sheet and coat thoroughly with salt. Pat the fish down to make sure the salt's sticking.

Step 4: Place the fish inside the cooler in a single layer, skin side down. Top this off with a layer of salt, and repeat until all the fish are in the cooler. Flip the top layer so the skin side is up. Finish off with a final, even layer of salt.

Step 5: Add a few wooden planks or dishes on top of the salt. Place the weights on top of the planks. As the salt draws moisture out of the fish, the salt will melt into a briny solution. You're adding the planks and weights to keep your precious fishes submerged as this brine starts to form.

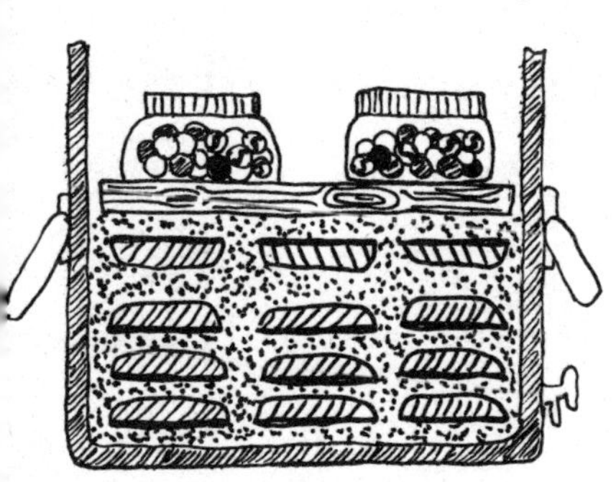

Step 6: Pop the lid on the cooler and let it sit for 2-3 weeks. The colder your climate is, the longer you'll have to wait.

Check your fish every couple days to make still they're still submerged in brine, and to add more salt to the solution. Don't forget this part! The fish can start rotting if the saturation level dips too much. Each time you add salt, put in enough so that no more will dissolve in the solution.

Do a smell test whenever you open up your cooler — you should smell fish, brine, and that's it. Grosser smells indicate something's gone wrong. The fish can be considered done (or phase 1 is, anyway) when the flesh is firm and translucent, and yields slightly when pressed. The fillets also might be a little smaller than when you put them in the cooler. If your fish stinks, is mushy, or is falling apart, toss it and scrub that cooler thoroughly with a baking soda paste.

PHASE 2: THE DRYING

Step 1: Prep a batch of fresh brine (make it about as salty as sea water) and pour it into a clean bucket. Dig the fish out of the vat and rinse them in the bucket to remove any excess salt.

Step 2: Transfer the clean fish to a flat surface and cover them with a new set of planks and weights. The pressing will squeeze out any remaining water in the fish and make air drying a lot quicker.

Step 3: Set up a wooden grate or frame (like a clothes-drying rack) in a dry spot outside. When the fish is no longer sopping wet, lay them over the frame in a single layer, flesh side up. Try to let as little of the fish touch

the wood as possible.

Let the fish stay here for a few days until each piece is thoroughly dry. Protect the fish from dampness as much as possible. That might mean moving the frame under an eave or into a ventilated shed during a rainstorm.

Fun fact: fish can get sunburn, even when they're dead. Too much sun can harden the fish's outer flesh and keep the inner flesh from drying properly. So if you can swing it, keep your whole apparatus partially shaded for the first day of drying, and then move it into direct sunlight for the rest of the drying process.

You can try this indoors if you need to, but keep in mind you need plenty of direct sunlight and serious ventilation.

When the fish is totally dry, pack it in an airtight container and either keep it in the fridge or a very cool, very dry place. If you have the means to vacuum seal the fish, so much the better.

how to make
Soap
without
burning
your
face
off

PLEASE READ

The process detailed in this zine requires a lot of care and attention. Some of the substances used to make soap are potentially very dangerous. Neither I nor the good folks at Microcosm can be responsible for you if you hurt yourself, someone else, or otherwise get into trouble. Please read all the instructions before you begin. Don't cut corners, especially with safety precautions — even if you've made soap before. Above all, take care of yourselves, and your friends, and have fun!

First, a history lesson...

Soap in its most basic form is created by combining some form of fat with a strong alkaline substance, a process called saponification. There are many theories about how humans got a handle on saponification. A popular legend is that soap was discovered in ancient Rome, on a mountain called Sapo. Maybe you've heard this? According to the story, when the fat from sacrificed animals ran down the side of the mountain to a river below, it mixed with the ashes from the burnt offerings and a crude soap formed in the river water. Thus the good people of Sapo were able to do their laundry.

While this story is really fun and creepy, it's not true. Nobody can find anything resembing Mount Sapo, and no one in Rome wrote about the phenomenon, either. Sorry, kids! I know how much you liked that gross story.* In reality, soap (in its modern formulation) has been in use all over the world since the early centuries of the Common Era. For most of that time, soap was made on a very small scale, and mostly used for laundry and household cleaning, as it was usually too harsh for bathing. Increasing awareness of hygiene and its ability to curb the spread of disease led to the large-scale industrial manufacturing of soap in the late 18th century. By the time the Industrial Revolution rolled (and in some places is still rolling) around, it was pretty normal to buy things instead of making them, and hand-made soap became more of a rarity. It's funny, then, that today "artisinal" soaps are a sort of fancy treat for people. Full circle!

*As an aside, can we please stop pretending that Romans invented everything? Give it a rest already.

About lye...

A few years ago I wrote a zine about nontoxic housecleaning. I didn't include any soap recipes in the zine because lye is quite poisonous and demands serious respect. It's kind of opposite of nontoxic. We all saw that movie. But I'm ready to talk about lye now, so here we go:

Lye is the lay term for a caustic alkaline compound, sodium hydroxide ($NaOH$). It is usually, though not always, the primary chemical used in making soap (potassium hydroxide is used to make liquid soap). Lye can be pretty intimidating for beginners, but alas, you can't make soap bars without it. Fortunately, it only takes a few precautions to keep things from getting hairy.

- Always buy 100% lye, and not drain cleaner, which usually consists of lye + a lot of other crap. You can find it at hardware stores - but bring your ID, some places restrict the sale of lye because it's used in meth production.
- When lye and water meet, they get very hot very quickly. You should know this, and you should know that the combination creates fumes you don't want to breathe. Always work in a very well-ventilated area. It's best if you can mix your lye and water outdoors; second best is to open a couple windows and point a fan out of one of them.
- Keep kids and animals out of your soapmaking area, including your lye-mixing area.
- Protect yourself by wearing safety goggles and thick rubber gloves. Long sleeves and close-toed shoes are also a good idea.
- Lastly, if lye gets on your skin, you can neutralize it by dousing your skin with vinegar. Keep a big bottle of vinegar around for this purpose.

Although it's possible to create soap using a single fat, most handmade soaps use a combination of oils. Each fat you'll encounter has a different assortment of fatty acids. Different fatty acids contribute to a soap's hardness, durability, lather, and moisturizing ability. The recipes in this zine will only use vegetable fats, but most commercial soaps are made with tallow. Tallow is rendered cow's fat. It's dirt cheap and creates a nice bar of soap, but there are so many other options to explore. The best soap has a good balance of hardening, lathering, and cleansing oils (see the handy chart to see which oils do what).

Hardening	Lathering	Moisturizing
palm *	coconut	olive
shea butter	castor	canola
jojoba	palm kernel*	soybean
beeswax	cottonseed (aka vegetable shortening - use organic, cotton plants are heavily sprayed)	sunflower
cocoa butter		rice bran
(lard + tallow)		safflower

SUPERFATS!
apricot kernel
sweet almond
avocado
kukui nut
wheatgerm

SUPERFATTING happens when there is a little more oil than lye in your soap. The extra oil ends up on your skin instead of getting saponified. Superfatting does two things:

① It makes your soap more lovely and moisturizing

② It ensures that your soap is mild enough. If there's too much lye in your soap it can be caustic; adding more oil gives you some wiggle room. In some books it might be referred to as "lye discounting."

You can use whatever oil you want for superfatting, including the ones you're already using in the recipe. But since you only need a little bit, why not try something nice?

The Process!

FIRST YOU NEED:

- a stockpot with handles (steel, enamel, or pyrex)
- a pyrex or heat-resistant plastic pitcher
- a glass mason jar
- a big mixing bowl
- two easy-to-read metal thermometers
- a scale
- two spoons (one plastic, one wooden)
- rubber gloves and goggles
- molds for the soap (see step 6)
- a towel or blanket
- emergency vinegar

all your oils, lye, additives, etc. See Recipes section!

1) Like most things, soapmaking goes smoothest if you have your shit together: measure all your ingredients beforehand and have your materials handy. Line your work area with newspapers and put on your gloves and goggles.

2) Take your pitcher, mason jar, lye and water to a well-ventilated area, outside if possible. Measure water into the pitcher and lye into the jar. Use a scale and measure by weight. Place both on a steady surface and attach a thermometer to the pitcher.

3) Add the lye to the water a little at a time and stir it with the wooden spoon until it's dissolved. Watch out - the water will get very hot, at least 200°. ALWAYS add lye to water, not the other way around. If you pour water on a heap of lye it will cause a teensy explosion. Put the pitcher in a safe place and let it cool to 110 degrees.

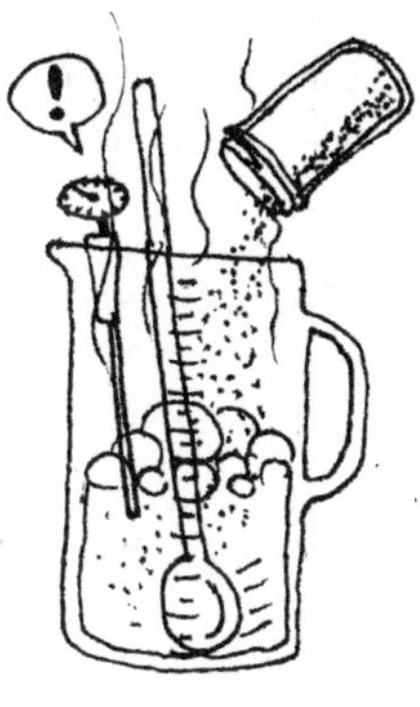

4) Weigh your fats in the plastic bowl, add them to the pot, and heat them to 110°. Watch the temperature closely. If you're using solid fats, weigh them in the pot and melt them before adding the liquid fat.

5) When lye has reached the same temperature as oil, add the lye mixture to the pot in a slow stream whilst stirring diligently. Have someone else put the lye pitcher in a safe place + keep stirring...

6) Annnd keep stirring! FOREVER. Here's the thing about soap: you have to stir it for a really long time, anywhere from 45 minutes to 3 hours. It's totally bearable if you have a few friends to help you. Another option, if you have a little money, is to buy a stick blender - more on that coming pages. In either case what you're looking for is soap thick enough to leave a trace behind when you run your spoon through it. This is appropriately called the trace stage.

7. When that sweet, sweet trace has been acheived, you can add your essential oils, scrubby bits, glitter, etc. Add fragrances first, exfoliants and textural bits second, and colorants last. Stir until everything is well blended but not too thick to pour.

8. Line your mold if it's not lined already. Use parchment paper and tape it down. A narrow wooden box is the best mold, especially if it has a lid. Another good option is a semi-flexible plastic container, which you can oil lightly instead of lining. Pour your soap into the mold and smooth the top with a spatula. Pick up the mold and drop it a couple of times to dislodge any air bubbles.

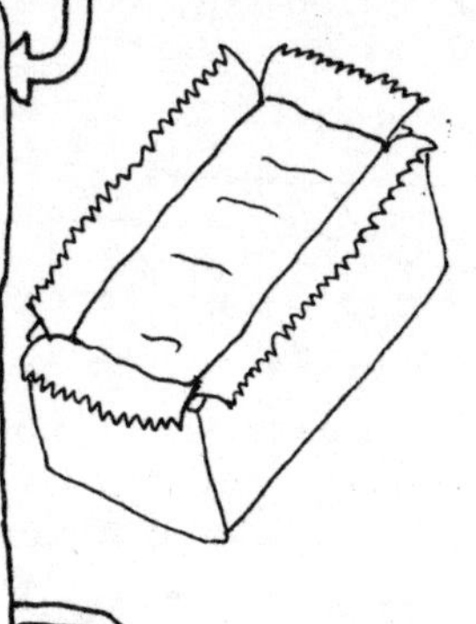

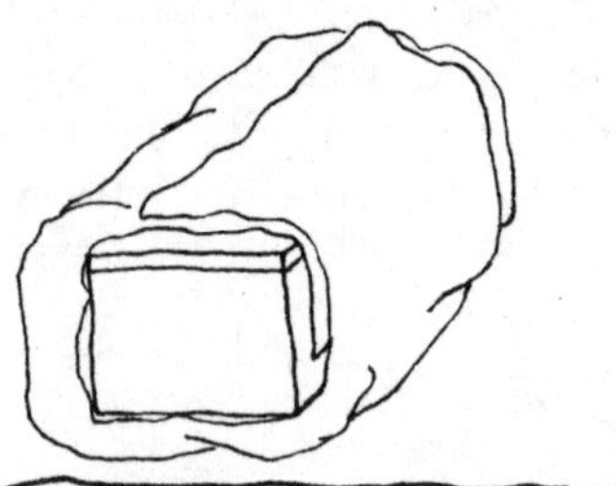

9. Time to put your soap to bed for a day or two. Put a lid on your mold, wrap the whole thing in a towel or blanket, and put it in a warm place. Leave it alone for 24 hours so it can cure. In the meantime leave your gloves on while you wash your equipment with hot, soapy water.*

After your soap has rested you can unmold it and cut it into bars; use a knife or a length of wire. Lay the bars out on a rack and let them dry out for a few weeks. Drying the soap will make it gentler and longer-lasting. If you try to use it right after you make it your soap will just melt in the shower.

If you really can't resist, at least wait a few days.

*But not your wooden lye spoon. It's gone forever. Sorry!

Special Tricks

• Using colorants: there are a few different tricks for coloring soap. Wax crayons actually work pretty well, but only certain colors of crayon. Cerulean is the best one to use, but yellow, orange, black and white work well too. Add up to a teaspoon of a spice to make nice warm, autumnal colors: turmeric makes a deep gold; paprika makes peach; cocoa powder makes a warm brown. The easiest way to make green soap is to start your batch with herb-infused oils. Comfrey leaf in particular is deep green and has skin-healing properties.

• Using additives: adding scrubby stuff like oatmeal or cornmeal to your soap invigorates your skin and makes your recipes more unique. Start with a cup of your chosen additive and add more if you need it. Plant bits like lavender buds and calendula petals are nice too, although they won't retain their colors through the soaping process. Sea salt and green clay are good additives for oily skin.

• Using a stick blender will bring your soap to trace very quickly, but you have to use it carefully. When you're adding your lye to your oils, use the blender as a spoon instead of turning it on. As soon as all the lye has been added you can start turning the blender on for five seconds at a time, stirring in between pulses. Your batch will thicken in just a few minutes, but resist the temptation to keep the blender humming - you don't want your soap to get too thick before you add your additives and scents in. If it does, you'll be stuck with boring soap, and it will be your own fault.

• Sometimes you might unmold your soap to find that a white layer of "ash" has formed on top. This is not a big deal: just cut or scrape it off and proceed!

Recipes

START HERE →

OR HERE ↓

Basic Soap Recipe #1

(Makes 5 pounds, or 48 bars!)

This recipe contains coconut oil for lather, olive oil for its emollient properties, and vegetable shortening to harden the bar. I added some cocoa butter to superfat the soap.

- 24 oz coconut oil
- 28 oz olive oil
- 24 oz shortening
- 4 oz cocoa butter
- 30.4 oz water
- 11.4 oz lye crystals
- ½ - 1 oz essential oil*

Basic Soap Recipe #2

(Makes 5 lbs, or 48 bars)

This recipe improves on recipe #1 with the addition of castor oil (for creamy lather) and canola and sunflower oils (for moisture).

- 20 oz olive oil
- 20 oz coconut oil
- 20 oz shortening
- 8 oz canola oil
- 8 oz sunflower oil
- 4 oz castor oil
- 21.7 oz water
- 11.2 oz lye crystals
- ½ - 1 oz essential oil*

* If you're using fragrance oil instead of essential oil, you can use a little more in your recipe.

Healing Soap for dry skin, eczema, upset skin

Use Recipe #2. A few days before you start, add 1 cup each comfrey leaf and calendula petals to the olive oil you're using. Strain all the solid bits out of the oil before you make soap. Use orange blossom or lavender oil (or both!) for fragrance.

Scrubby Soap for dirty hands

Use Recipe #1. After you hit the trace stage, add ½ cup each cornmeal and oatmeal to your soap. Use a citrus oil like lemon or bergamot for fragrance. If you want to, add a teaspoon or more of turmeric for color.

Oatmeal Soap for itchy skin

Use Recipe #2. Replace the water in the recipe with rose petal tea. Use chamomile and rose oils for fragrance (don't use chamomile if you are allergic to ragweed). Add up to a cup of coarsely ground oatmeal.

Femme Soap

Use Recipe #1. Replace the water in the recipe with rose petal or jasmine flower tea, or use flower-infused oils. Add some glitter during the additive stage and color with 1 teaspoon of paprika for a nice peachy color. For scent, use rose*, jasmine, rose geranium, neroli, or ylang-ylang essential oil.

Good Morning Soap

Use either recipe. Use peppermint tea instead of water. After trace stage, add ½ c each sea salt and sand or pumice powder. Make sure to use clean, fine sand. Add basil and peppermint oils for scent.

Sleepy Soap

Use either recipe. After trace stage, add up to a cup of lavender flowers. Use chamomile and rosemary oils for scent + soothing properties.

Swirly Soap

If monochromatic soap is too boring for you, add some visual interest with a nice swirly pattern. If you've ever tempered an egg-based sauce, it's basically the same process. If this interests you, read on:

When it comes time to add colorant, scoop out about a cup's worth of soap. Add your colorant to this little bit, mix it well, and then drizzle the colored soap back into the pot. Hold the cup a few inches from the bowl so you don't get too much in one place. Swirl the soap gently with a rubber spatula to achieve desired marbling.

* use rose perfume oil, rose essential oil is crazy expensive

Food Preservation Resources

How to Store Your Garden Produce: The Key to Self-Sufficiency
by Piers Warren
Totnes: Green Books, 2008

Ball Complete Book of Home Preserving: 400 Delicious and Creative Recipes for Today
edited by Judi Kingry and Lauren Devine
Toronto: Robert Rose, 2006

The Canning, Freezing, Curing & Smoking of Meat, Fish & Game
by Wilbur Eastman
Charlotte, VT: Garden Way Pub Co, 1975

Wild Fermentation: The Flavor, Nutrition and Craft of Live-Culture Foods
by Sandor Ellix Katz
White River Junction, VT: Chelsea Green Pub Co, 2003

I have people to thank! Give it up for: Lacey Clemmons, Corinne Manning + Kathryn Higgins for their editorial guidance; Kim Reinauer for her canning expertise; ZAPP and its volunteers, both past and present; the Seattle Public Library, as usual; and my man Greg Brown, as always.

About the Author

R**aleigh Briggs** is a bodyworker, mother of two, and the best-selling author of *Make Your Place: Affordable, Sustainable Nesting Skills,* and of several other books and zines on DIY culture. She lives in Seattle.

PESTS UNITE!
MICROCOSM PUBLISHING.COM

MORE BY RALEIGH BRIGGS FROM www.MICROCOSM.PUB

FIX
Your
HOME
THE
SUSTAINABLE
ART OF PATCHING,
PLUMBING,
AND REPAIRING
raleigh
briggs

chapter 1
how to make
Soap
without
burning
your
face
off
raleigh briggs

herbal
first
aid
(assembling
a natural first
aid kit)
(ARNICA)

avoid
dangerous
chemicals!
so clean!
so
damn
nice &
clean
nontoxic
housecleaning